GEOGRAPHY OF THE WORLD

THE LURE OF
MOUNTAIN
PEAKS

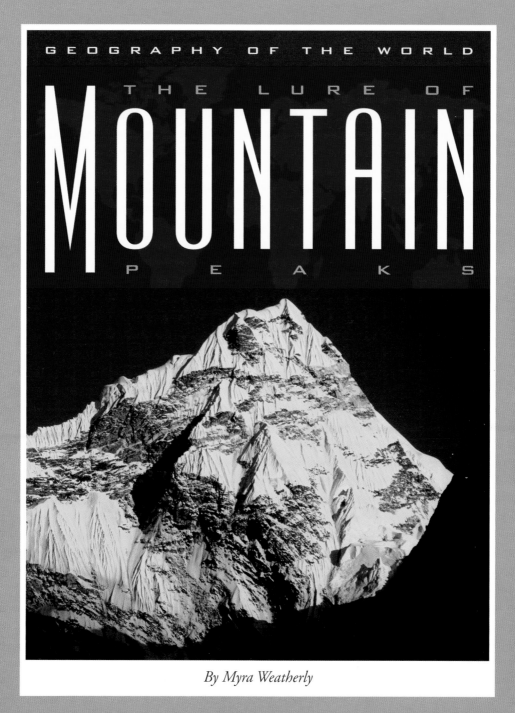

By Myra Weatherly

THE CHILD'S WORLD®
CHANHASSEN, MINNESOTA

The Child's World

Published in the United States of America by The Child's World®
PO Box 326, Chanhassen, MN 55317-0326
800-599-READ
www.childsworld.com

Content Adviser:

Mark Williams,

Associate Professor,

University of Colorado,

Boulder, Colorado

Photo Credits: Cover/frontispiece: Galen Rowell/Corbis.
Interior: Animals Animals/Earth Scenes: 17 (Henry Ausloos), 23 (Mark Jones), 26 (Johnny Johnson); Corbis: 5 (Hulton-Deutsch Collection), 6 (Alison Wright), 9 (Bettmann), 11 (David Keaton), 12 (Tim Davis), 13 (Yann Arthus-Bertrand), 16 (Torleif Svensson); Burt Glinn/Magnum Photos: 4; Craig Lovell/Corbis: 8, 15; Galen Rowell/Corbis: 14, 18, 20; Hubert Stadler/Corbis: 21, 22; Travelsite/Global/Picture Desk: 24.

The Child's World®: Mary Berendes, Publishing Director

Editorial Directions, Inc.: E. Russell Primm, Editorial Director; Melissa McDaniel, Line Editor; Katie Marsico, Associate Editor; Judi Shiffer, Associate Editor and Library Media Specialist; Matthew Messbarger, Editorial Assistant; Susan Hindman, Copy Editor; Sarah E. De Capua and Lucia Raatma, Proofreaders; Marsha Bonnoit, Peter Garnham, Terry Johnson, Olivia Nellums, Chris Simms, Katherine Trickle, and Stephen Carl Wender, Fact Checkers; Tim Griffin/IndexServ, Indexer; Cian Loughlin O'Day, Photo Researcher; Linda S. Koutris, Photo Selector; XNR Productions, Inc., Cartographer

The Design Lab: Kathleen Petelinsek, Design; Kari Thornborough, Page Production

Library of Congress Cataloging-in-Publication Data
Weatherly, Myra.
　The lure of mountain peaks / by Myra Weatherly.
　　p. cm. — (Geography of the world series)
　Includes index.
　ISBN 1-59296-333-1 (library bound : alk. paper)
　1. Mountains—Juvenile literature. I. Title. II. Series.
　GB512.W43 2004
　551.43'2—dc22   2004003716

Table of Contents

CHAPTER ONE

4 Reaching the Top

CHAPTER TWO

6 Mount Everest: The Roof of the World

CHAPTER THREE

12 Mount Kilimanjaro: Africa's Tallest Mountain

CHAPTER FOUR

17 Mont Blanc: The Highest Alp

CHAPTER FIVE

21 Aconcagua: The White Sentinel

CHAPTER SIX

24 Denali: The Great One

28 Glossary

29 A Mountain Peaks Almanac

30 The Mountain Peaks in the News

31 How to Learn More about Mountain Peaks

32 Index

CHAPTER ONE

REACHING THE TOP

People have always been drawn to mountain peaks. Mountaintops often seem mysterious, and reaching them is a challenge.

Japanese monks view a mist-covered Mount Fuji. This peak is considered sacred and is surrounded by several temples.

Long ago, people believed that gods lived in the high mountains. These ancient people sometimes ventured up mountains to leave gifts for their gods. In the 19th century, mountain **summits** began to attract scientists. They wanted to study the mountains, to learn how they formed and what kinds of plants and animals lived there. By the end of the century, people were climbing high peaks for the thrill of it.

The lure of mountain peaks has not faded. Today, many people enjoy mountain climbing, though it remains a

Three climbers attempt to cross the Alps in 1866. Even in modern times, mountain climbing demands courage, can be dangerous, and is almost always thrilling.

dangerous sport. In 1988, Stacy Allison became the first American woman to stand at the top of Mount Everest, the highest peak in the world. After this climb, she said, "I realized that in the end, every summit boils down to what you're willing to risk to pursue your passions and make your dreams come true."

CHAPTER TWO

MOUNT EVEREST: THE ROOF OF THE WORLD

The top of Mount Everest is the highest point on earth. It rises 29,035 feet (8,850 meters) on the border between Tibet and Nepal. Viewed from afar, the peak is dazzling on a sunny day. But up close, it looks very different. The top of Everest is in fact a land of wind-blasted snow, ice, and rock.

To understand how Mount Everest formed, you have to know a little bit about the earth's structure. Earth's outer layer, called the crust, is not made up of one giant piece. Instead, it has cracks, like a giant jigsaw puzzle. Earth's

THE TALLEST IN THE SOLAR SYSTEM

Olympus Mons, a mountain on Mars, towers 15 miles (24 kilometers) above the red planet's surface. It is three times the height of Mount Everest.

Since 1852, people have acknowledged Mount Everest as the world's tallest peak. Strong winds, bitter temperatures, and sheer height also make it one of the most difficult to climb.

crust is made up of about 20 of these huge puzzle pieces, which are called plates. These plates are slowly moving.

Mount Everest is part of the Himalayan mountain system. Like the rest of the Himalayas, Everest started forming about 50 million years ago. The

EVEREST, THE MOUNTAIN AND THE MAN
Mount Everest is named after Sir George Everest, who was a British official in India in the middle of the 19th century. He was the first Westerner to record the location and height of Everest. Tibetans, on the other hand, call the mountain Chomolungma, which means "goddess mother of the world."

plate carrying India, then an island, moved slowly north and crashed into the Asian Plate. When the two plates collided, earth's crust crumpled and folded. The folds pushed upward, forming peaks and valleys. Over time, Mount Everest was born. The plate movement that created Everest is still happening. Even today, this giant mountain is moving northeast at a rate of 2 inches (5 centimeters) a year, about the rate that your fingernails grow.

The Khumba region on the slopes of Mount Everest is home to the Sherpa people. This region is crisscrossed with rocky trails. Sherpas usually travel on foot up and down these trails, sometimes loaded down with heavy packs. Do they need a road system? The Sherpas tell Westerners: "We are Sherpas. We walk."

Many Sherpas cling to their old ways. Families survive by raising yaks and planting potatoes. They depend on the shaggy yak for heavy work. There are more than 50 types of yaks. These beasts also provide Sherpas with many things they need. The yaks' hair is used for clothing. Tents can be made from the hide. The yak is also a source of meat, milk, and butter.

Early on, climbers from the West recognized the skill and

In addition to helping travelers make their way across the Himalayas, Sherpas also farm potatoes, raise yaks, and weave wool.

hardiness of the Sherpas. When people first tried to reach the summit of Everest in 1922 and 1924, they used Sherpas as **porters.** More people tried to climb Everest in the 1930s and 1940s.

Tenzing Norgay (left) and Edmund Hillary display their medals after being honored for their climb by the Nepalese king in 1953.

By 1950, many people had unsuccessfully tried to reach the peak of Everest. Some people thought it was impossible. But then on May 29, 1953, a Sherpa named Tenzing Norgay and a beekeeper from New Zealand named Edmund Hillary stepped onto the summit. They were the first to make it to the top of the world. Norgay later wrote: "I picked up two small stones and put them in my pocket to bring back to the world below."

Since the 1980s, more and more people tried to climb Everest. But it remains a difficult task. Climbers may face fierce winds, avalanches, sudden snowstorms, and hidden **crevices.** They have to carry tanks of oxygen because the air at the top is so thin that it makes people sick. To this day, only about 1,300 people have made it to the summit of Mount Everest. More than 150 people have died trying.

The many Westerners who try to climb Everest have made tourism an important part of the local economy. But while these tourists bring

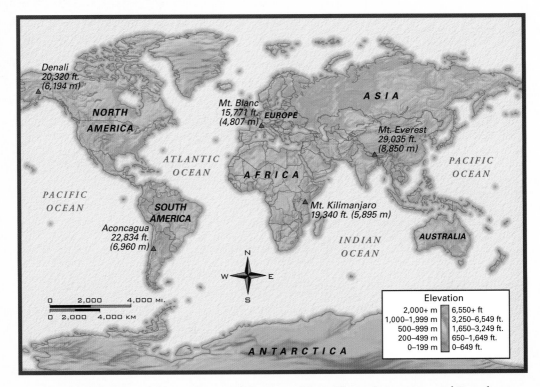

A map of Mount Everest, Mount Kilimanjaro, Mont Blanc, Aconcagua, and Denali

Modern-day climbers reach the summit of Mount Everest. In addition to expeditions such as the one shown here, recent climbing trips have been organized to remove litter from the peak.

jobs, they also damage the environment. People in Nepal and Tibet and around the world are working to protect Everest. Their efforts include restrictions on cutting trees and the establishment of Sagarmatha National Park in Nepal.

People are concerned with what might happen to Mount Everest as the number of climbers steadily grows. But one thing is certain. People will continue to risk their lives for the thrill of reaching the highest point on earth.

CHAPTER THREE

MOUNT KILIMANJARO: AFRICA'S TALLEST MOUNTAIN

Snowcapped Kilimanjaro rises in Tanzania, about 200 miles (320 km) south of the **equator.** At 19,340 feet (5,895 m), it is the highest peak in Africa. It also ranks as the world's tallest freestanding mountain. Kilimanjaro is not part of a mountain range. Instead, it rises majestically from a rolling plain.

Elephants in Kenya peacefully pass by Mount Kilimanjaro. Three inactive volcanoes make up this mountain.

Kibo is the youngest and highest of Kilimanjaro's three volcanoes.

Kilimanjaro is a **dormant** volcano. But it could erupt again.

The mountain began forming between 2 million and 3 million years

ago when hot rock, or **magma**, burst up through earth's crust. In

time, the lava retreated, leaving a cone of ash around the rim.

Glaciers atop Kilimanjaro have also helped shape its summit.

Today, the glaciers and snowfields that have covered the peak for

11,700 years are melting. Some scientists think the glaciers may be

A climber carefully makes his way up the slopes of Mount Kilimanjaro.

gone by the year 2020. Earth's rising temperatures may account for the massive melt.

The Chagga people live on the rich volcanic soil around the base of Kilimanjaro. They tell stories of demons and evil spirits living on the mountain.

These evil spirits were supposed to be guarding treasures of silver. For centuries, the Chaggas had no desire to climb the mountain and discover if the stories were true. Today, however, Chaggas work as guides and porters for climbers from around the world.

In the mid-1800s, climbers first attempted to scale Kilimanjaro. In 1889, two Europeans, Hans Meyer and Ludwig Purtscheller, became the first people to top the rim. Meyer later recalled, "The icefields flashed and glittered in the dazzling sunlight."

Kilimanjaro now attracts about 20,000 trekkers each year. During the climb, hikers travel through five different climate zones. As a Chagga guide says, "It's like walking from the equator to the North Pole in only a week."

Fields and villages blanket the lower slopes of Kilimanjaro. In this region, Chaggas grow crops such as coffee and bananas. Between 6,000 and 9,000 feet (1,800 and 2,750 km) is **rain forest**. Here trees, vines, flowers, giant ferns, birds, and butterflies abound. Leopards, lions, and colobus monkeys also live in the dense forest.

Huts such as the ones shown here are common to Tanzanian villages along the lower slopes of Kilimanjaro. Tanzania is home to more than 35 million residents.

Amboseli National Park is located at the base of Mount Kilimanjaro and serves as a habitat for animals ranging from lightning-fast cheetahs to gigantic elephants.

Above 9,000 feet (2,750 m), giant heather and tall grasses begin to break up the thick forest. At about 11,000 feet (3,350 m), the grasses give way to high desert. In this region, volcanic rocks pepper the ground. Finally, at 19,340 feet (5,895 m), climbers reach the summit. Up there, the temperature is below freezing, the ground is covered with ice, and the views are spectacular.

Parts of Mount Kilimanjaro are now a national park. People are working to preserve its fragile environment. It is hoped that people far in the future will be able to enjoy the amazing beauty of "the shining light."

CHAPTER FOUR

MONT BLANC:
THE HIGHEST ALP

For centuries, people gazed at Mont Blanc with fear. A 16th-century myth claimed the mountain was a prison. According to the legend, the devil was imprisoned on the peak after losing a battle with Saint Bernard, a Christian monk.

The myth about the mountain began to unravel in the 18th century. In 1760, Swiss physicist Horace-Bénédict de Saussure offered

Scenic Mont Blanc is the highest peak in Europe.

Mont Blanc has become a popular European tourist attraction for sightseers, skiers, and determined climbers such as the ones shown here.

a prize to whoever could discover a route to the top of Mont Blanc. Two Frenchmen, Michael-Gabriel Paccard and Jacques Balmat, finally claimed the prize in 1786. De Saussure climbed the mountain himself a year later. He wrote, "Imagine a deep cavern, the entrance to which is a vault of ice. . . . Looking up, an immense glacier crowned by pyramids of ice can be seen."

Mont Blanc is the highest peak in the Alps, rising 15,771 feet (4,807 m) along the border between France and Italy. About 65 million years ago, the collision of the African and Eurasian plates caused earth's crust to fold, creating the

Alps. Some of this folding caused the crust to crack. As a result, molten rock welled up and formed high peaks, including Mont Blanc.

The top of Mont Blanc is covered with ice. One of the peak's most spectacular icefields is Mer de Glace, which means "sea of ice" in French. It is the second-longest glacier in the Alps. Mer de Glace stretches about 3.5 miles (5.6 km) on the northern slope of Mont Blanc.

Climb Mont Blanc and you'll see more than just rocks and glaciers. At the base of the mountain are meadows where deer and ibex graze. Moving up the slopes, the meadows give way to forests of larch and fir. Plants such as edelweiss, wild orchids, and buttercups grow on rocks as high as 13,000 feet (4,000 m). Higher up, crows and golden eagles soar across the skies.

OTZI THE ICEMAN

In 1991, a frozen body was discovered in a melting glacier high in the Alps. Scientists soon determined that the body was 5,300 years old. At first, they thought that the "ice man," nicknamed Otzi, had frozen to death. But tests in 2003 showed that he probably died after a big fight. He had an arrow wound in his back. And he had blood from four different people on his knife, his cloak, and an arrow. Who knows what other frozen secrets remain hidden in the Alps?

Over the years, more and more tourists and mountain climbers have come to Mont Blanc. During the 20th century, many farmers and ranchers became guides and innkeepers. Today, modern transportation hurries people through the Mont Blanc region. One of the world's longest automobile tunnels runs through the mountain. The Mont Blanc tunnel is 7.5 miles (12 km) long. And higher on the mountain, cable cars make it easy for climbers, skiers, and sightseers to visit.

Many people worry about what tourism is doing to Mont Blanc.

Are you afraid of heights? If the answer is yes, then riding in a cable car high above the ground might not be for you. Since the early 1900s, cable cars have helped tourists to travel uphill in the Alps.

Because it is so easy to reach, many people climb the mountain. Sometimes as many as 200 people are at the summit at the same time. With so many people tramping up and down Mont Blanc, it is important that both hikers and public officials do everything they can to preserve the beautiful mountain.

CHAPTER FIVE

ACONCAGUA:
THE WHITE SENTINEL

Aconcagua is the highest mountain peak in South America.

It is also the highest mountain in the world outside of Asia.

This wedge-shaped mountain of rock and ice is part of the Andes

Mountains. It rises 22,834 feet

(6,960 m) in western Argentina.

As mountains go, the Andes are

quite young. Millions of years ago,

AN ANCIENT NAME
The Inca people called the mountain Ancocahuac. The name comes from the words *anco* ("white") and *cahuac* ("sentinel"). A sentinel is a soldier who stands guard. Because the snowcapped Aconcagua looms over every-thing around it, "white sen-tinel" is a good name for it.

Many people consider Aconcagua to be the highest peak in the Western Hemisphere.

A visitor peers down at Incan ruins near Mendoza, Argentina. The Incan culture dates back nearly 600 years.

the South American Plate began colliding with the Nazca Plate in the Pacific Ocean. This collision caused earth's crust to fold. It also produced a lot of volcanic activity. Aconcagua was formed by this volcanic activity.

The Inca people lived in the Andes before Europeans arrived in South America. No one knows if any Incas ever climbed to the top of Aconcagua. But scientists have found Incan sites very high on the mountain.

In 1897, Swiss mountain guide Matthias Zürbriggen became the first person known to climb to Aconcagua's summit. The first American to reach the peak was author James Ramsey Ullman in 1928. He later wrote that Aconcagua's "**altitude** is so great, its cold so bitter, its storms so frequent and savage, that the ascent ranks among the most grueling ordeals known to climbers."

The Aconcagua Provincial Park was created to conserve the mountain's landscape, plants, animals, and Incan sites. Woody bushes and stunted grass grow in the park. More than 60 types of birds live in

There are two species of condor. Andean condors such as the one shown here make their homes in South America. As their name implies, California condors live in the state of California and have a slightly shorter wingspan than their South American relatives.

the area, including the Andean condor. Condors are the largest birds in South America. Their wings are almost 10 feet (3 m) across. The park is also home to mountain rats, red fox, and many snakes and lizards.

In the 1980s, Aconcagua became a popular peak to climb. The increased traffic damaged the mountain environment. The number of climbers may have to be limited to help protect the plants and animals that live there. Perhaps only this will help preserve the environment of the "white sentinel."

CHAPTER SIX

DENALI: THE GREAT ONE

Denali is the highest mountain in North America. It rises to a height of 20,320 feet (6,194 m). Located in Alaska just below the Arctic Circle, it is also one of the coldest peaks in the world.

Long before Europeans discovered the glacier-studded mountain, Native Americans roamed its slopes. They called it Denali, which means "the great one."

Snow-capped Denali was named by the Athabascan Indians, who continue to live in Alaska today.

In 1794, English navigator and explorer George Vancouver spotted "a stupendous snow mountain." He was the first Westerner known to have seen Denali. William Dickey was searching for gold when he first saw the mountain in 1896. He later wrote, "We named our great peak Mount McKinley, after William McKinley of Ohio, who had been nominated for the Presidency."

Right away people protested the name change. A clergyman and explorer named Hudson Stuck led the first successful climb of Mount McKinley in 1913. Afterward, he worked to restore the mountain's original name. In 1980, the state of Alaska changed the mountain's name back to Denali, but the national government continues to call it Mount McKinley.

Denali began forming some 65 million years ago, as two of earth's giant plates were grinding against each other. This movement thrust up huge

THE DENALI LEGEND
A Native legend explains how Denali formed. According to this story, huge waves rolling in from the sea threatened an Indian warrior named Raven. To protect himself, Raven threw a spear at them. When the spear hit, the wall of water became solid, forming the Alaska Range. The greatest wave became Denali.

amounts of material. Wind and water wore this material away, and huge masses of ice weighed it down. The result was Denali.

Today, Denali sits in the middle of the Denali National Park and Preserve. The park, which covers 6 million acres (2.4 million hectares), remains largely wild and unspoiled. A huge number of animals make their homes in the park. These include grizzly bears, timber wolves, Dall sheep, moose, caribou, and many kinds of birds.

Dall sheep live in bitterly cold mountain regions in Alaska and western Canada.

Spruce forests blanket the mountain's lower slopes. Higher up the mountain, no trees grow. Here **tundra** replaces forests, and mosses, sedges, and lichens hug the ground.

The opening of Denali National Park brought more people into Alaska's northern reaches. They visit Denali to watch the wildlife and go backpacking, skiing, and mountain climbing. Some people even take plane rides to get a good look at the dramatic mountain.

Denali is a magnificent mountain, and it attracts fearless mountain climbers. But its location and many avalanches make it a difficult climb. Only about half of the people who attempt to reach the summit succeed. In the last 60 years, 91 people from 13 different nations have died trying to climb the mountain. Denali will always challenge even the world's best climbers.

HIGH ALTITUDE RESCUE

On June 4, 2003, a National Park Service helicopter made a daring rescue on Denali. A climber named Camilo Lopez was sick and was located more than 19,000 feet (5,900 m) above the ground. The helicopter hovered above Lopez and dropped a rescue basket. Lopez secured himself in the basket. The helicopter then flew down the mountain with Lopez hanging below. He was taken to a hospital in Anchorage, Alaska, where he recovered.

Glossary

altitude (AL-ti-tood) Altitude is the height of an object above the surrounding ground. At high altitudes, the thin air can make people sick.

crevices (KREV-iss-ez) Crevices are long, narrow cracks in the surface of the earth. Hidden crevices are a danger to mountain climbers.

dormant (DOR-muhnt) If something is dormant, it is not active at that time. Kilimanjaro is a dormant volcano.

equator (i-KWAY-tur) The equator is an imaginary line around the middle of earth, halfway between the North Pole and South Pole. Kilimanjaro lies near the equator.

glaciers (GLAY-shurz) Glaciers are large sheets of moving ice. As glaciers move, they wear away the rock beneath them, reshaping mountains.

magma (MAG-muh) Magma is melted rock within the earth. Kilimanjaro began forming when magma burst through earth's crust.

porters (POR-turz) Porters are people who are hired to transport baggage. Sherpas acted as porters to the first people who tried to reach the summit of Mount Everest.

rain forest (RAYN FOR-ist) A rain forest is a region that gets a lot of rain and usually has a very wide variety of plant and animal life. Part of Kilimanjaro is covered with rain forest.

summits (SUHM-itz) Summits are the top points of mountains. The first people to reach the summit of Mount Everest, the highest point on earth, were Tenzing Norgay and Edmund Hillary.

tundra (TUHN-druh) Tundra is a treeless region in the upper reaches of a mountain. Mosses and lichens grow in the tundra.

A Mountain Peaks Almanac

Mount Everest
Height: 29,035 feet (8,850 m)

Continent: Asia

Country: Nepal and Tibet

Parks and preserves: Sagarmatha National Park

Mount Kilimanjaro
Height: 19,340 feet (5,895 m)

Continent: Africa

Country: Tanzania

Parks and preserves: Kilimanjaro National Park

Mont Blanc
Height: 15,771 feet (4,807 m)

Continent: Europe

Country: Italy and France

Parks and preserves: None

Aconcagua
Height: 22,834 feet (6,960 m)

Continent: South America

Country: Argentina

Parks and preserves: Aconcagua Provincial Park

Denali
Height: 20,320 feet (6,194 m)

Continent: North America

Country: United States

Parks and preserves: Denali National Park and Preserve

The Mountain Peaks in the News

65 million years ago	Denali starts to form when two of earth's plates move against each other.
50 million years ago	Mount Everest, along with the rest of the Himalayas, begins to form.
1760	Swiss physicist Horace-Bénédict de Saussure offers a prize for the discovery of an access route to the top of Mont Blanc.
1786	Michael-Gabriel Paccard and Jacques Balmat ascend to the top of Mont Blanc and claim de Saussure's prize. De Saussure makes his own ascent the following year.
1794	English navigator and explorer George Vancouver spots Denali.
1865	Mount Everest is named after Sir George Everest, the British surveyor-general of India from 1830 to 1843.
1889	Europeans Hans Meyer and Ludwig Purtscheller top the rim of Mount Kilimanjaro.
1896	Gold prospector William Dickey sights Mount Denali and decides it should be named after William McKinley; protests ensue.
1897	Swiss mountain guide Matthias Zürbriggen makes the first recorded ascent to Aconcagua's summit.
1913	Clergyman and explorer Hudson Stuck and his three companions climb to the summit of the south peak of Mount Denali.
1953	Edmund Hillary and Tenzing Norgay become the first people to reach the summit of Everest on May 29.
1980	The state legislature of Alaska changes the name of Mount McKinley back to Denali, though it remains Mount McKinley on national documents. The park and preserve are also changed to Denali National Park and Preserve.
1988	Stacy Allison becomes the first American woman to stand at the top of Mount Everest.
2003	A National Park Service helicopter is used to rescue Camilo Lopez, who was stuck at a height of more than 19,000 feet (5,800 m) on Denali.

How to Learn More about Mountain Peaks

At the Library

Corral, Kimberly, and Hannah Corral. *My Denali: Exploring Alaska's Favorite National Park with Hannah Corral.* Portland, Ore.: Graphics Arts Center Publishing Co., 1995.

Dubois, Mark, and Cathy East Dubois. *Ice Mummy.* New York: Random House Books for Young Readers, 1998.

Ratter, Charles. *The Towering Sentinels: Mountains.* Mankato, Minn.: Creative Education, 2003.

Wallace, Holly. *The Mystery of the Abominable Snowman.* Chicago: Heinemann Library, 1999.

On the Web

VISIT OUR HOME PAGE FOR LOTS OF LINKS ABOUT THE MOUNTAIN PEAKS:

http://www.childsworld.com/links.html

Note to Parents, Teachers, and Librarians: We routinely verify our Web links to make sure they're safe, active sites—so encourage your readers to check them out!

Places to Visit or Contact

DENALI NATIONAL PARK AND PRESERVE
PO Box 9
Denali Park, AK 99755

EMBASSY OF ARGENTINA
1600 New Hampshire Avenue NW
Washington, DC 20009

FRENCH GOVERNMENT TOURIST BUREAU
610 Fifth Avenue
New York City, NY 10020

KILIMANJARO NATIONAL PARK
PO Box 96
Marangu, Tanzania

NEPAL TOURISM BOARD
Tourist Service Center
Bhrikuti Mandap
Kathmandu, Nepa

Index

Aconcagua, 21–23
Aconcagua Provincial Park, 23
African Plate, 18–19
Allison, Stacy, 5
Alps, 18
Andean condor, 23
Andes Mountains, 21
animal life, 15, 19, 23, 26
animals, 8
Argentina, 21
Asian Plate, 7

Balmat, Jacques, 18
Bernard (saint), 17

cable cars, 20
Chagga people, 14, 15
condors, 23
crust, 6–7, 18–19

Denali, 24–27
Denali National Park and
    Preserve, 26, 27
Dickey, William, 25

environmental damage, 11, 23
Eurasian Plate, 18–19
Everest, Sir George, 7

farming, 15
formation, 6–7, 13, 19, 22,
    25–26
France, 18

glaciers, 13–14, 18, 19, 24

Hillary, Edmund, 9
Himalayan mountain system, 7

icefields, 19
Inca people, 21, 22
India, 7
Italy, 18

Khumba region, 7
Kilimanjaro, 12–16

Lopez, Camilo, 27

magma, 13
McKinley, William, 25
Mer de Glace icefield, 19
Meyer, Hans, 14
Mont Blanc, 17–20
Mont Blanc tunnel, 20
Mount Everest, 5, 6–11
Mount McKinley. *See* Denali.

Native Americans, 24, 25
Nazca Plate, 22
Nepal, 6, 11
Norgay, Tenzing, 9

Otzi ("ice man"), 19
oxygen, 10, 11

Paccard, Michael-Gabriel, 18

plant life, 15, 16, 19, 23, 27
plates, 7, 18–19, 25–26
porters, 9, 14
Purtscheller, Ludwig, 14

rain forests, 15
Raven (Indian warrior), 25

Sagarmatha National Park, 11
de Saussure, Horace-Bénédict,
    17–18
scientists, 4–5, 13–14
Sherpa people, 7–8
South American Plate, 22
Stuck, Hudson, 25
summits, 4–5, 9, 10, 13, 16, 20,
    22, 27
Swahili people, 12

Tanzania, 12
Tibet, 6, 11
tourism, 10–11, 20
tundra, 27

Ullman, James Ramsey, 22–23

Vancouver, George, 25
volcanoes, 13, 22

yaks, 8
Yeti, 8

Zürbriggen, Matthias, 22

About the Author

Myra Weatherly's love for mountains began in her child-hood. Growing up in the foothills of South Carolina, she was never far from mountains. Though not a climber, she counts as one of her fondest memories a trip (by rail) up the Jungfrau in the Alps. She has even ventured down into a glacier. Weatherly writes for children and young adults. This is her third book for The Child's World.